VICT RY?!

Brain Tumors and God's Coincidences

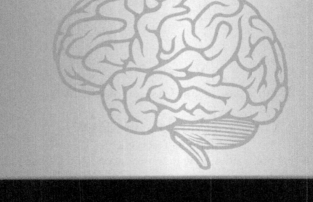

Judy Lombardo

www.EnhancedDNAPublishing.com
DenolaBurton@EnhancedDNA1.com
317-537-1438

Victory?!
Brain Tumors and God's Coincidences

Cover Design: Rachel Anthony and Marvin Rhodes, Jr.
Author Headshots: Chandra Lynch – Ankh Productions

ISBN-13: 978-1-7369079-2-4
Library of Congress Number: 2021913153

DEDICATION

This book is dedicated to everyone who reads it and gets a glimmer of hope, humor, or insight from it.

December 2021

MERRY CHRISTMAS

To my cousin Julia
with all my love!

Judy

Judy Lombardo

INTRODUCTION

I originally titled this, *Victory?! (some names have been changed to protect the guilty)*. That was back in 2012 when I wrote it as a one-woman Fringe show for IndyFringe. The performance had to be forty-five to sixty minutes in length, no more and no less. In 2013, I revamped the show for ChiFringe (in Chicago) but kept the same name. In 2016, I made it into a multi-media performance when I took it to Hollywood Fringe. (The best nine days of my life!), but I still kept the same name. Then in 2019, I wrote and performed *Victory?! Again,* which added new stories, but I still kept the same subtitle, *(some names have been changed to protect the guilty).*

When I went to organize the best of each version of the play into a book format, I intended to keep the subtitle. Then my publisher said to me, "Your subtitle doesn't tell what the book is about." She recommended that it should be changed. So, I reread the book I wrote and thought, "What is it about?" I knew it was about my life as a two-time brain tumor survivor, but I found there was a recurring theme in it, that I hadn't planned on: coincidences. Some would call them signs from above or life's coincidences, but I chose the words "God's Coincidences" because one of the most incredible coincidences is church related and there is no way all the other coincidences could have happened without the intervention from a higher power.

Let me explain what I mean by recurring coincidences. The most recent one happened a couple of weeks ago. I received a timeline from my publisher saying what date we expect this book to be released. The following day I received a phone call from my neurosurgeon's office, telling me it was time for my check-up MRI and that they would schedule the MRI and follow-up visit with the neurosurgeon, and then call me with the date. Guess what date my appointment was scheduled for? The same date as this book is scheduled to be released. What are the odds???? I didn't have any say in what day either was scheduled. Also, the neurosurgeon didn't know I was writing a book, nor did the publisher know I had biennial MRIs. Coincidence.

At first, I thought this was a cool coincidence, but as I write this, I admit I'm scared. I always get nervous before my biennial MRI. I'm not afraid of the MRI itself. Many people are claustrophobic and afraid of spending 40 minutes inside the machine. I am not. I'm nervous about the results. It took several years, but I learned to not think about the possibility of my condition worsening for 2 years at a time. I only worry about it around MRI time. If the doctor tells me the MRI shows the current tumor has not changed in shape or size, I'm relieved and think, "Yay! I just bought myself another 2 years." However, a year ago, when I had my biennial MRI, the neurosurgeon thought it was stable but said it looked like there could be some growth on it. So, he didn't want to wait two years. He wanted to see me "in about a year, to be cautious." At the time, I didn't have any clue I had written enough material for a book, nor did I know how to contact a publisher and convince them to take on my book. But here I am, excited that my first book is being published and yet wondering if I've gotten it done just in time to face another round of surgery, radiation or worse. I am grateful for all the additional years I have been given and sadly think of those who lost their lives way too young due to brain tumors and brain cancer. Yet, I want more time.

But we must have a positive attitude when possible. It is okay to break down, as long as we then turn around and build back up. Remember that, no matter what struggle you are facing.

At the end of each chapter, you will find two pages titled, "Your 'Victory?!' Notes." These are for you to use as a journal for yourself, or maybe not use them at all. For example, if you are going through a stressful experience, of any kind, you may wish to write how the previous chapter applies to your life. But no matter what you do with those pages, I hope this book impacts your life in a positive way.

TABLE OF CONTENTS

CHAPTER 1

A JOLT LIKE NO OTHER

Picture it: Indianapolis, October 1992, A twenty-five year old woman is sitting in her office's lunchroom, WHEN SUDDENLY A BRICK COMES FLYING IN AND SMACKS HER IN THE BACK OF THE HEAD! Well, that's what it felt like anyway. I was so dizzy, I didn't know which way was up. I thought I was going to pass out, so I put my head between my knees. But it didn't help. I felt like I was turning summersaults over and over and then sometimes it felt like I was tumbling sideways like a bowling ball headed for the gutter. There was a woman sitting next to me, but I don't remember who it was. But I remember the look on the face of the woman sitting across the room from me. She was just staring at me with a terrified look on her face. Like she couldn't imagine what was going on, but we both knew it was very bad! I moved slowly and quietly the rest of that day and the next, like I would if I were trying to fight off the flu. But two days later, again in that same lunchroom, **WHAM**! This time I put my head down on the table. When the spinning and pressure stopped, I went to my desk and called the doctor. They saw me after work **that day**. The doctor told me that I had fluid in my left ear and an inner ear infection. They sent me home with a decongestant and antibiotic. But…I was only satisfied with this diagnosis, until that evening. I was sitting on my couch at home watching TV and I felt like I was constantly moving. I described it to the doctor as feeling like I was riding the waves on a raft. I was told that since I had fluid in my ear it was possible that could happen and to just keep taking my medicine for ten days. But this feeling of motion only occurred when I was sitting – not lying down or standing up. However, I continued to take my medicine as the doctor directed, and every night I sat on that couch and felt like I was on an amusement park ride, and I WANTED TO GET OFF!

Ten days later, I went back to the doctor and told her that I did not feel any better. Again, she looked in my ears and saw just a little fluid, so she gave me 10 more days of medication. After the second set of ten days, I went back to the doctor and told her I STILL wasn't feeling any better. She said that my ears were clear now and they couldn't figure out what was wrong, so they wanted to send me to a neurologist. But it was a week before Thanksgiving and I was supposed to fly home to Connecticut in a few days, and no one could see me until December 2nd. So, they scheduled my appointment with the neurologist and said that I should definitely NOT fly, just in case there was still extra fluid in my ears that they couldn't see. They told me, if you fly when you have fluid in your ears, it is excruciatingly painful. So, they scheduled me for an MRI. They did my MRI on the Tuesday before

Thanksgiving. My friend David had to drive me, and I was too sick to care that I was in a claustrophobic machine. My parents suggested that I take a bus to Pittsburgh and they would pick me up there.

YOUR "VICTORY?!" NOTES

YOUR "VICTORY?!" NOTES

CHAPTER 2

THE KINDNESS OF STRANGERS

"Excuse me, do you know where…?" I asked someone as they walked past me in the Columbus, Ohio bus station. "Where is the nearest payphone?" I asked another person. I finally found someone to answer my question and they pointed in a different direction. "Over there, thank you," I said. I walked over to the pay phone picked up the receiver, and pumped quarters into the phone. Then I dialed the push button pay phone.

"Hello, may I please speak to Dr. Theodora?" Long pause and I had to hold my hand over the ear not being held up to the phone just to hear. "This is Judith Lombardo, she asked me to call her by 6pm today." Longer pause and I put more quarters into the phone as I got more anxious. "Hello, Dr. Theodora? What did the MRI show? *(Listening)* A mass? You mean I have a cyst in my brain near my ear? *(Listening)* A tumor? You mean that I have a brain tumor? What do I do? *(Listening and nodding my head)* Okay, an appointment with a neurosurgeon. December 4th. Okay. Thanks. Bye." I hung up the phone in a daze.

After that phone conversation in the Columbus, Ohio, bus station, I went outside and stood in line waiting to reboard the bus for Pittsburgh. I was in a daze when one line over a college aged man got off the bus and said to me, "Excuse me, you were on our bus weren't you?" I looked at him and I looked at where I was, and I suddenly realized I was about to get on the wrong bus! So, I walked over and reboarded the bus where this stranger was, and found my overnight bag in the seat. I thanked him and the three other guys traveling with him.

I don't know if at that point I was more scared about having a brain tumor or the prospect of ending up alone in a strange bus station at midnight.

YOUR "VICTORY?!" NOTES

_____

_____

_____

_____

_____

_____

_____

_____

_____

_____

_____

_____

YOUR "VICTORY?!" NOTES

_____

_____

_____

_____

_____

_____

_____

_____

_____

_____

_____

_____

_____

_____

Judy Lombardo

CHAPTER 3

THE NEUROSURGEON – #1

The first neurosurgeon I saw was sitting in the center of the exam room holding a multi-piece model of the brain. He began, "Now, Miss Lombardo, what I would do is make a window in the skull, behind the left ear like this. Then I would move the left side of the brain over like this and go straight to the center and (a piece of the brain model fell on the floor) oops, uh, remove the tumor. Now, the nerves in there are just millimeters thick or even less and of course the brain controls all bodily functions, including whether you are breathing or your heart is beating. One small slip could mean permanent damage or even death." He looked up at us and tried to put the model back together, while pieces kept popping out and he continued to get more and more flustered. "Do any of you have any questions," he asked. Then answering my dad's question, he continued, "Well, we probably won't need to shave the entire head. We will just shave the back left quarter of the head." He kept juggling the pieces trying to put the model brain back together when another piece dropped out. "Now, um, uh, if we need to…" I don't remember the rest of what he said because I started laughing. I interrupted him, "Doctor, I'm sure you can put me back together better than you can put that model back together. And dad, who cares if they shave my head, I just want to live!"

Both of my parents were there with me during that visit. The whole time that the neurosurgeon was trying to put the model back together, my dad was getting more and more annoyed and my mom just kept staring at him quizzically. But I honestly thought it was funny. It didn't make me any more nervous than I already was, and I had FULL confidence in this doctor. But, I don't know why.

YOUR "VICTORY?!" NOTES

_____

_____

_____

_____

_____

_____

_____

_____

_____

_____

_____

_____

_____

YOUR "VICTORY?!" NOTES

_____

_____

_____

_____

_____

_____

_____

_____

_____

_____

_____

_____

_____

_____

Judy Lombardo

CHAPTER 4

THE NEUROSURGEON - # 2

I decided to get a second opinion just to be safe. A few days later my mom and I were in another neurosurgeon's office. An old man in a lab coat entered the room trembling and said, "Good morning Miss Lombardo, I'm the head neurosurgeon here at the hospital. Uh huh, uh huh." He offered his hand out to shake mine and continued, "I understand you have a Meningioma, benign, that needs to be removed." (*He was still trembling.*) "Well don't worry; we'll get you taken care of. No problem. Uh huh, uh huh. Sure, it is not easy *(Still trembling)* on you, but for the doctors this is a piece of cake and you will be fine afterward." Then he patted me on the back, for reassurance I suppose.

Now what the HELL do you think was going through my mind at that point? My outward facial expression may have been a plain staring face. But on the inside my facial expression was mouth wide opened and one eyebrow raised. But I kept a blank stare on my face. My mom was a pro! She acted like it was any other doctor visit. When we left, mom asked me if I wanted her to drive and I said, "YES!" As we drove away, just to make sure we were far enough from the hospital and the doctor was nowhere around, I slowly looked over my right shoulder and then just to make double sure, I slowly looked over my left shoulder and then I lost it. Yelling and all in one breath I said, "What the hell kind of surgeon is that?! How can he operate on anyone or any body parts, let alone my brain? I can just see him shaking through the whole thing." I took three deep breaths as my mother said calmly, "So, you are going to go with the first surgeon then?" I was flabbergasted! Was she kidding? How could she be so calm? So, I started in again, yelling and all in one breath, "What the heck do you think I'm saying? Of course, I'm going to go with the first surgeon! How could I even consider this other surgeon? I don't care if he has a great reputation. He is not working on my brain!"

YOUR "VICTORY?!" NOTES

_____

_____

_____

_____

_____

_____

_____

_____

_____

_____

_____

_____

_____

_____

YOUR "VICTORY?!" NOTES

_____

_____

_____

_____

_____

_____

_____

_____

_____

_____

_____

_____

_____

_____

_____

Judy Lombardo

CHAPTER 5

THE STRANGENESS OF FRIENDS

My friend Paulina is a very sweet person and an intelligent one. In fact, I know that I would have never gotten through this whole ordeal without her. However, on occasion, Paulina has been known to say some pretty silly things. For example, she was the first person to make a strange comment to me about my situation. One night I was talking to her on the phone, expressing my angst about my diagnosis to her, when Paulina said, "Well, Judy, you sure have a lot of people praying for you. It's a good thing most of your friends are Catholic". To which I yelled, "What difference does that make?! It's not even a true statement!" Paulina responded, "Oh, I..I..I don't know what I'm saying. People just don't know what to say to you. You should write down all the funny things people say to you and keep the list for future humor." Well Paulina, you got your wish!

Steve was my best guy friend in college. Now, Steve is of Polish descent and yes, you do need to know that to understand this story. At the time of my diagnosis, it was suggested to me that I have several people I knew well, donate blood for me, in case I needed it during the surgery. Steve offered to donate for me. After he donated, he called me and said, "Well, Judy, I just donated blood for you and you'll know if you get my blood." *(Long Pause)* "And how will

I know that?" I asked quizzically. Steve said, "If you get my blood, you'll wake up from surgery craving a Polish sausage!" Huh????

Take that any way you want folks. I never asked him what he meant.

My college roommate, Felicia, said to me one day, "Ohhhh, I just can't wait until this whole thing is over!" SHE COULDN'T WAIT?!

And my church choir director. Professionally he was a family counselor – and again, you do need to know this to find the humor in this story. When I told him about my diagnosis he panicked and said, "Geez, it's like everyone should get their head examined!" Of course, he meant physically examined, not in the emotional sense as he did at his day job. The ironic thing here is that four years later, his youngest sister, at the age of twenty-five, would be diagnosed with a glioblastoma multiforme; which is usually the deadliest form of brain cancer. But we'll talk more about that, later.

Our church pianist said to me, "Don't worry about anything. You are a wonderful person and bad things don't happen to wonderful people." Seriously? What am I, a five-year-old?

Ah, and the lovely Miss M. who worked with me at the insurance company. She came up to me one day at work and asked me if they were going to have to shave my head for the surgery. I said, "Oh, I don't even care!" She said, "You're right. Who cares what your hair looks like when you're dead!" And she walked away.

But the most shocking incident came right after my surgery.

A couple of days after surgery when I was awake enough to talk with my family, my mom brought me some cards that people sent and said, "When we got back to your apartment after the surgery your neighbor and his girlfriend had left us a plate of homemade chocolate chip cookies and a card. When you are up to eating, I'll bring you the cookies, and you can see the card when you get home." I thought this was odd since she had brought other cards to me, but I quickly dismissed it.

A couple of days later, still in the hospital, I asked mom about the card again. And again, she said, "You can see it when you get home." Hmmmmmm…something wasn't right. So, when I arrived home, ten days after surgery, you can bet the first thing I said was, "Okay mom, so where is this elusive card?" "On the table," she said dismissively. I walked over to the table, found it, opened it and received the shock of my life! It was addressed to "The Lombardo Family" and it was a SYMPATHY CARD!!!! My neighbor hadn't even waited to find out if I survived the surgery!

Judy Lombardo

YOUR "VICTORY?!" NOTES

_____

_____

_____

_____

_____

_____

_____

_____

_____

_____

_____

_____

_____

YOUR "VICTORY?!" NOTES

Judy Lombardo

CHAPTER 6

FAITH

My mother stayed with me in my Indianapolis apartment for most of December 1992. One weekend at church they announced they were having an Advent confession opportunity the following week. I hadn't been to confession in years. My mother said to me, "I think you should go to confession. I think it will make you feel better if you do that before your surgery. I'll go too." My heart sunk. I felt that was her way of saying, "I want you to go to confession before your surgery, just in case you die." She never said that, but that's how I felt. Somehow I knew she was right. We went on a Thursday night. There were many different priests at several places throughout the church, so you could go to any one of them. I don't know why but I chose to get in line to speak to a very thin 6' 6" tall priest. Maybe I chose him since he obviously stuck out. I confessed and my mom made sure that I was set to receive the "Sacrament of the Sick" before my January 4th surgery. I had always known that sacrament as "Last Rites" and thought they changed the name just so I wouldn't panic. Later a doctor friend of mine told me that the sacrament name had been officially changed to "Sacrament of the Sick" because so many more people survive serious illnesses these days. That was a relief to me.

Two days before my surgery, my mother, father, sister and I went to church together. They were all in Indy for my surgery, and we were all staying in my large, but only one-bedroom apartment. We hadn't done that since I had been a few months old. It's funny how life can be cyclical like that. But I digress. When we arrived at church we found out that the priest I had known and trusted, had suddenly left the priesthood. "He did that after he told me specifically he would be there to give me Sacrament of the Sick," I thought. I was shocked and scared. But, of course, that wasn't about me. It had been sudden, so there was a visiting priest saying mass that day. Fortunately, my father explained my situation to the visiting priest and he said he would give me the sacrament right after mass. Now I was more nervous than ever about my surgery.

However, after mass, the visiting priest, whose name I never remembered, came to me with the holy oil (at least I think that's what it was, I don't really remember). He talked to me gently saying that looking at me he couldn't believe how sick I was. "I feel fine," I told him, as if that would give reason for me not to have my big surgery. I was nervous and felt like I was shaking as he blessed me. Then the strangest thing happened. A sense of calm overcame me. My head was clear and I suddenly felt like everything was going to be okay. It was a great relief to me. I didn't understand why I felt relieved. From then on, right up to the time of surgery I was 100% calm. We went out to dinner that night and I enjoyed it and enjoyed friends visiting with me the next day.

The day of the surgery I was so calm, although I admit to not sleeping much the night before. I was up once an hour and my mom kept telling me to get back into bed because she thought my body needed rest before it went through this ordeal. I might have gotten five hours of sleep, while waking up each hour. Paulina chose to go and sit with my family at the hospital while I was having the surgery. I chose to ride with Paulina to the hospital. "My family is driving me crazy," I told her, as I jumped in her car and my mother was still insisting that I ride with them. I told Paulina to drive. My mom, dad and sister followed in their car. They didn't know where the hospital was, and we didn't have GPS then.

At the hospital, I changed into my gown for surgery and they did a clotting test. Basically, they used a cookie cutter like object to perforate a two-inch spot on my arm. I clotted immediately. The nurse told me that was a very good thing. Hmmmmmm...It hadn't occurred to me that I might not clot after surgery. Yikes!

As they wheeled me from my room toward the operating room, Paulina, my sister, and my mom (in that order) hugged me and wished me luck. Then my dad came running up to me, kissed me and said, "Good-bye sweetie." I sat straight up on the moving bed! "What?! What do you mean good-bye?" Then I immediately became calm and said, "No dad, it's going to be okay. It's just 'see you in a couple of days'." Yep, I still felt that unexplainable calm.

YOUR "VICTORY?!" NOTES

YOUR "VICTORY?!" NOTES

CHAPTER 7

WAKING UP & GOING HOME

On January 4, 1993, just before they put me under anesthesia, I looked at the clock in the O.R. It said 8:30, a.m. that is. When I first woke up after surgery, I could see through blurred vision a clock on the wall in front of me. It said, 11:30. But I didn't know if it was a.m. or p.m. or the same day or what. I couldn't keep my eyes open for very long but I heard a nurse say, "She's waking up." Then they asked me my name, if I knew where I was and what day it was. All my answers came out slightly slurred with my eyes still closed and one...word...per... breath. But I HEARD AND UNDERSTOOD EVERYTHING! I remember a nurse asking my neurosurgeon, "It has been twelve hours and she is not fully awake. Is she okay?" He replied very calmly, "We will just have to wait and see." WHAT? I was panicked internally. I wanted to yell, "Yes, I'm here! I'm awake! I can hear you. I just can't speak or open my eyes!" I was scared and I didn't want them to give up on me! But there was nothing I could do.

About an hour or so later I think, I opened my eyes because

I felt a presence hanging over me. It was my friends, David and Sheila. Now, they always teased me about when my birthday was, because I had a friend that I had known for a very long time that got my birthday wrong every year. She always thought it was a day earlier than it really is. David thought it would be funny to ask me, while I was still under the anesthetic, when my birthday was. Without opening my eyes, and one word per breath I said, *"Month…date… you…crazy…turkey…buzzard."* I am happy to say that he has been called that nickname ever since!

Sometime in the next ten days the hospital priest brought me communion. Guess who it was? That 6'6" tall man (Father Dave) that had listened to what I thought was going to be my last confession. Just one more sign that God was in control. Incidentally, fifteen years later at my new church, Father Dave was assigned to be our Associate Pastor. Just one of God's coincidences. I am still amazed by this fact.

So, after a ten day stay in the hospital I got to go home. You know what the best thing about going home was? Getting to sit in a bathtub and shaving my legs! It had been almost two weeks since I was able to bathe normally or shave my legs. It was a GLORIOUS feeling! Seriously!

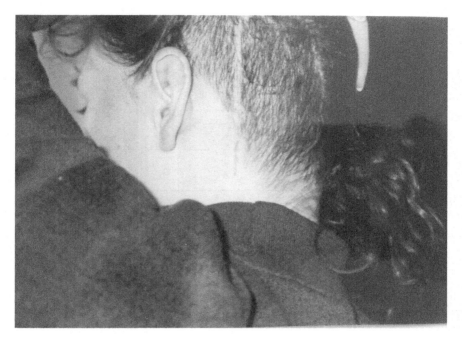

My surgery scar, three weeks after my first surgery!

YOUR "VICTORY?!" NOTES

_____

_____

_____

_____

_____

_____

_____

_____

_____

_____

_____

_____

YOUR "VICTORY?!" NOTES

Judy Lombardo

CHAPTER 8

HERE WE GO AGAIN

Six years later, round two began just as round one had, with those same severe dizzy spells. I was at lunch with a friend at a restaurant, when it hit me, and I knew. I just knew. The tumor was back. So, I called my <u>new</u> family doctor. She got me in IMMEDIATELY. I went into her office; she examined me and had the nerve to tell me that I had fluid in my left ear. I just glared at her. She said, "I know what you are thinking. You think that you have another tumor." "I'm sure of it," I said, nodding my head. She said, "But you do appear to have fluid in your ear. Take the decongestant and antibiotic, and I promise this time I won't let you go so long without an MRI. If you don't feel better in ten days let me know and I'll get you in to see your neurosurgeon." "Okay," I said. I left with my prescription, knowing I would be back. Yep, ten days later I was back. She sent me for an MRI and to see my neurosurgeon, and guess what? He confirmed that there was a new tumor growing right where the old one had been.

Going back to work that day, after that appointment, I was in a daze crossing the street thinking, "OMG, this disease really is what is going to ultimately do me in." I was about a third of the way across the street, when a car sped by me almost running over my toes! I can still feel the breeze on my face and I curl my toes every time I think of it! But then I stopped, right there in the middle of the street and thought, "Or I could get hit by a car today, and not even make it to the radiation!" We never know, do we?

YOUR "VICTORY?!" NOTES

_____

_____

_____

_____

_____

_____

_____

_____

_____

_____

_____

_____

YOUR "VICTORY?!" NOTES

_____

_____

_____

_____

_____

_____

_____

_____

_____

_____

_____

_____

_____

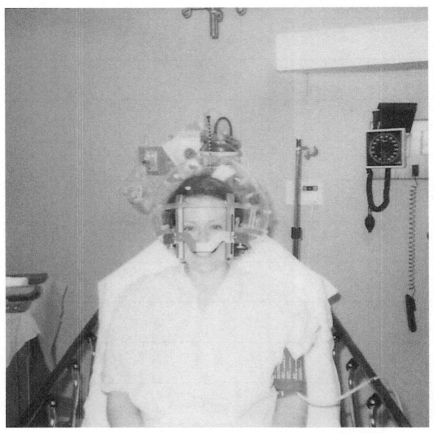

Photo taken by Indiana University Health nurse in June, 1999.

CHAPTER 9

RADIATION

Yep, that's me about to receive Gamma Knife Radiation in June of 1999. The Gamma Knife center nurse took this picture saying, "We take two pictures of you. One you can keep and the other is for identification purposes." IDENTIFICATION PURPOSES??? What does that mean? Won't I be able to identify myself to you when this is done??? I wanted to ask those questions, but I never did.

Gamma Knife surgery involved three doctors: a radiation specialist, my surgeon and a physicist. My physicist looked like Albert Einstein! Just like all those pictures you see of Albert Einstein with his white frizzy hair sticking out. It was funny, and yet scary to think they needed Albert Einstein to get through this procedure.

My neurosurgeon came in and gave me four shots of an anesthetic in a square formation on the top of my head. This is where they inserted the screws to hold the head frame in place. Next, they fitted a half dome plastic piece, that contained one hundred and two holes in it, onto the head frame. Next came an aluminum dome on top of the plastic dome. It too, had one-hundred and two holes in it, and it had gears on either side of it. They took an MRI of me with this all attached to my head. "It's aluminum so it doesn't conflict with the MRI," they assured me. After the MRI, the physicist dialed in the coordinates of the location of my tumor by turning the gears on each side of my aluminum dome. The idea of the Gamma Knife is to send the strongest amount of radiation to the tumor to kill the cells, without damaging any healthy tissue around it. After they dial the coordinates in, they put your head in a "microwave". Well, that's what it felt like. It was a box and felt and sounded like a hollow cave. Then the radiation doctor and Albert Einstein went into another room with a big glass window and administered the radiation for thirty-five minutes.

"You won't know if it worked for months or even years," they told me. "It is considered successful if the tumor never changes in size or shape as shown on yearly MRIs." It was successful.

In the meantime, I had some strange side effects and didn't realize they were from the radiation. I had been told to stay out of the sun for a year after the radiation. So, for the next three months I did. Then on Labor Day that year, I wanted to get some sun. It was a beautiful three-day weekend and I chose to lay out by the pool. I kept my head in the shade because I knew I wasn't supposed to get the radiated part of me in the sun. It just never occurred to me that having my arms and legs in the sun, while wearing sunscreen, would cause a problem.

After the three-day weekend of carefully sunning myself, I went back to work. I was out walking at lunchtime and felt this awful friction on the back of my legs rubbing against the work pants I was wearing. When I got back to the office, I went in the ladies' room and found that the back of my upper legs had a one-inch-thick lesion covering each of them. It was bizarre! It looked like something out of a Bugs Bunny cartoon! All I could think of was, "What did I sit in at the pool, this weekend?" I could barely get my pants back up because my upper legs were so swollen in the back. After I got home, I examined it more carefully and with a mirror. What was it?

The next couple of days I wore long skirts to work because the lesions kept getting thicker and harder, so my business casual pants didn't even fit. I finally called the doctor. This was the "new family doctor" from the previous chapter, that was sure I didn't have a second brain tumor. Anyway, I went to her and told her I'd never seen anything like it. She said, "You had that radiation procedure, didn't you?" Just then, I remembered being told not to go out in the sun for at least a year after radiation. But they never told me why or what might happen. She thought this was an allergic reaction to the combination of the sun and the radiation. I was treated with oral steroids. The thick lesions went away slowly over the next month or so. I assure you that to this day, I stand or sit in the shade as much as possible!

Please understand that I am not trying to talk anyone out of having radiation treatments of any kind deemed necessary for them. I'm still glad I had the Gamma Knife radiation since it stopped my tumor growth. I just realized that it is important to closely follow all guidelines that the medical professional provides.

YOUR "VICTORY?!" NOTES

_____

_____

_____

_____

_____

_____

_____

_____

_____

_____

_____

_____

YOUR "VICTORY?!" NOTES

_____

_____

_____

_____

_____

_____

_____

_____

_____

_____

_____

_____

_____

_____

_____

Judy Lombardo

CHAPTER 10

BALANCING ACT

One of the permanent effects this has had on me is; without warning the left side of my face goes numb. And I don't feel a change in my face, so often I spill liquid out the left side of my mouth when drinking. That is, drinking even NON-alcoholic beverages. I figure that to the average person I just look clumsy, but that is not the case.

After nearly 15 years of dealing with fatigue due to the tumor and more so from the radiation, I decided one day that I finally felt well enough to start doing activities outside of work. I started reading at church and doing local theater. One day, someone at church said to me, "You have an excellent speaking voice. Would you like to be a reader? We could use more of them." Excellent idea, I thought. I love public speaking. I accepted and they conducted the orientation for the role. After my first time reading, as I went to step down from the altar I mentally froze and panicked. I WAS SCARED STIFF! You see, since my first surgery, I had double vision in my left eye. It had greatly improved over the years, but then, and even today, sometimes, when I look

57

down to walk downstairs, I cannot always distinguish one step from another. Therefore, I ALWAYS held onto railings or another person when walking downstairs. Now, for the first time in many, many years, I had to learn to walk downstairs without holding onto anything. I was so upset that first day after I had to do this, that I cried all the way home. All I could think of was, just when I thought I was getting back to normal, I couldn't even be a reader at church. How depressing! Thankfully, the carpet in the church has four lines leading off the altar. If I adjust my view of the three steps so that each line looks like it is on a different plane on each step, I can descend the steps safely. To THIS DAY, I still adjust my view of the line in the carpet on the steps to descend the altar.

I started doing local theater in 2009 and 2010, with no issues. Then in 2011, I was cast in the largest role I'd ever been given. I was the main supporting actress in a show at Buck Creek Players. I was so excited to be doing it! There was one part in the show where we did a square dance. You know, Do-Si-Do, swing your partner and the whole bit. Now, I had to deal with another permanent issue that resulted from the tumor: losing my balance. By opening night, I had learned to run in heels - down one set of steps across the stage and up another. Then came the swing your partner part of the dance. I managed to figure out how to deal with being swung around once and then having to run off the stage. It wasn't easy and my head felt awful, but I did it for each performance. Then, on the second weekend of performances my dance partner communicated to me, on stage and in front of an audience, "Let's go around twice tonight." Noooooooooooooooo is what went through my head at that second. I knew I'd fall down if I was swung around twice with no break. I quickly communicated, "ONCE!" to my partner and that's all he did. Phew!

Later in 2011, just two nights before the opening of a show I was in, I developed vertigo. I had it all the time, not just if I spun around. I immediately started taking my medicine and sat upright and quietly on the couch for twenty-four hours. No dress rehearsal for me. Opening night, I found they had somewhat adapted the set, just for me. Instead of one of the other characters sitting, they had me sit for a lot of the show. Then the director told me, "Judy, if you get dizzy on stage, don't panic. Just work it into the show. Say something like, 'Oh, all this excitement is getting to me, I have to sit down,' and then sit down wherever you are, until it passes." That quelled all my fears! This director showed me that my health condition did not have to keep me from doing what I loved! Now, I am happy to report that I have NEVER had to use that mechanism – not for that show, or ever since. Yet.

YOUR "VICTORY?!" NOTES

_____

_____

_____

_____

_____

_____

_____

_____

_____

_____

_____

_____

_____

_____

YOUR "VICTORY?!" NOTES

Judy Lombardo

CHAPTER 11

SURVIVOR GUILT

S urvivor guilt. Have you ever heard of it? It is a real psychological condition and I had it, I just never knew there was a name for it.

Shortly after my first surgery, I decided that since I had survived, God must have kept me on this planet to help create more brain tumor survivors. I still remember the DESPERATE feeling I had when I was first diagnosed. It was DESPERATION to fight, to live.

A few years after my first surgery, I had my first opportunity to help someone. It was my former church choir leader's youngest sister. By this time, I had married into the family so they were a large part of my life now. Jackie was about 25 at the time, just as I had been when I was first diagnosed. However, Jackie was diagnosed with a glioblastoma – which is usually the most lethal of all brain cancers. She was told her tumor was inoperable, and she was given about 3 weeks to live. Her immediate family sat around crying and saying, "It must be God's will." Now, I personally feel that there is a fine line between God's will and free will, and that we never know where that line is, until we use all of our God-given resources, including our common sense! I gave Jackie's family my surgeon's name and phone number and my parents gave her parents lists of books they found helpful when they researched the subject after my first diagnosis. Finally, one of her sister's made a phone call and they eventually got her to a surgeon who would operate. Jackie lived a full year and she had a reasonably good quality of life – painting the house and going to Colts games. The first Christmas after Jackie was diagnosed, her family visited with my in-law's and their family and they just kept staring at me. They didn't speak to me. They barely nodded their heads hello to me when they came in, even though we were all sitting in the same living room. It was a very eerie and uncomfortable feeling for me sitting in that room and all of them talking about IT, but no one talking to me or with me. During the next nine months of Jackie's life, my own marriage was going downhill - for other reasons. My husband and I were going to marriage counseling at the time of Jackie's death. I remember being in the marriage counselor's office and telling the counselor that my husband and his family were constantly questioning me about my headaches, and my fatigue and claiming that they always happened during family events and that it wasn't fair to my husband, "Jackie did this…" and "Jackie never had to do that…" they would say. I grant you that the migraines and fatigue befell me during family events, BUT they also happened at all other times too! This was the way my body reacted to the brain tumor and brain surgery. I was thrilled just to be alive! I remember my husband telling the marriage counselor that Jackie never had fatigue; she had energy and did lots of activities. So, if she could do it, I must be faking it. In shock and hyperventilating, I yelled, "BUT JACKIE DIED!!!!"

My marriage ended a few months later.

My advice to survivors of all types – no matter what type of devastating event it is: an illness, an accident, abuse or anything else: NEVER ALLOW ANYONE, EVER, TO MAKE YOU FEEL AS IF YOU SHOULDN'T HAVE LIVED OR YOU DIDN'T SUFFER ENOUGH!

YOUR "VICTORY?!" NOTES

_____

_____

_____

_____

_____

_____

_____

_____

_____

_____

_____

_____

_____

YOUR "VICTORY?!" NOTES

Judy Lombardo

CHAPTER 12

JOHN, JOHN, LUKE AND JULES

John Belushi, John Candy, Luke Perry and Jules Smith. If that was the answer to a Jeopardy question, the proper response would be, "Who are four people who died on my birthday?" Well, John Belushi died on the day of my birthday party, but the coincidence is still eerie.

When I heard that fifty-two-year-old Luke Perry died on my fifty-second birthday, I had another moment of survivor guilt. But that lasted only a few moments until I heard that the lovely young lady, known simply as Jules, passed away that day too. For over a year, she suffered with a glioblastoma that she was diagnosed with just before her eighteenth birthday.

While she suffered, she also thrived in life and taught so very many people about the joy of living. She was a beautiful person and a beautiful soul, and I was privileged to meet her one December day, in a place where neither of us lived, but fate, or God put us together.

I met Jules' mother first, coincidentally on Facebook. Two

years earlier I had reconnected with a high school classmate who then lived in Colorado. We friended each other on Facebook. On January 1, 2018, my high school classmate posted, "It's the first day of a new year and my new calendar says to post, *What is something you have done that you think none of my other Facebook friends have done?*" So, I responded, "I survived two brain tumors, wrote a one-woman show about it and have performed it in Indianapolis, Chicago and Hollywood." Someone then tagged Jules' mother on the post and said, "Look at this! Contact her." And that is how this friendship began.

I was so impressed by her mother. This woman had researched everything and done everything I knew possible, in less than a month after her daughter was diagnosed. Jules went home after brain surgery on her eighteenth birthday. She went through rounds of chemo, and always had a smile on her face. I followed the journey of this beautiful, innocent young woman on the internet.

One day her mother posted that they were going to Duke University to participate in a clinical trial over Christmas. What a coincidence! I was going to Raleigh/Durham too, to visit my sister who lived there. I asked if I could meet Jules since I was going to be there at the same time they were. Her mother said, "Yes". I met this peaceful, young, nineteen-year-old woman and her mother at the Ronald McDonald house in Durham, NC. We talked for about an hour. Jules asked about my play and she told me that she was a musician that sang and played in a band. I got to see pictures of her singing with her band. Jules even wrote music! She asked if I would let her write music for *Victory?!*. I told her I would love that. We planned that we would work on that long distance when she started feeling better.

Well, that didn't happen. She briefly thrived after the clinical trial and then got much worse and passed away on my birthday. It stinks! It isn't fair! Something needs to be done!

YOUR "VICTORY?!" NOTES

YOUR "VICTORY?!" NOTES

_____

_____

_____

_____

_____

_____

_____

_____

_____

_____

_____

_____

_____

_____

Judy Lombardo

CHAPTER 13

DOGS AND BRAIN TUMORS

As I said earlier, I figured out that my purpose in life was to help others survive such an ordeal. But it never occurred to me that I was destined to have two dogs with a similar ailment.

My first dog Bailey was diagnosed with Cushing's Disease at the age of 9. In case you are wondering, Cushing's Disease is a tumor under the brain. It was surreal, as they say. It never occurred to me that I would have a dog with a brain tumor. My sweet Bailey lived to be 13. She had some extremely costly medication for 4 years. But I loved her so much and I would do it again.

My second dog, Daisy, was a stray I took in. She barely lived to be four years old. Guess why? Yes, she too had a brain tumor.

I don't know why or how these two dogs were sent to me to take care of them. But I learned a lot more about brain tumors than I ever wanted to know.

Perhaps I really was the best person to be their human, due to their condition. I don't understand it and it still perplexes me.

My third dog, Charlie, passed away recently at the age of ten and a half. He died of a heart condition, not a brain tumor.

YOUR "VICTORY?!" NOTES

_____

_____

_____

_____

_____

_____

_____

_____

_____

_____

_____

_____

_____

YOUR "VICTORY?!" NOTES

Judy Lombardo

CHAPTER 14

EATING MY WORDS

I am a game show junkie especially for word games. I always have been. Growing up, the show "Password" in its various forms and with its various hosts was my favorite. So, when I heard that it's last host, Bert Convy, died, suddenly, I was shocked. It was New Year's Eve, December 31, 1991, and I was hanging out at my friend David's house watching TV. They listed celebrities that had passed away that year and Bert Convy was one of them. I said to David, "Hey, I heard this a couple of months ago. How did Bert Convy die?" David replied, "A cancerous brain tumor." I said, "Oh my gosh, that's awful, because YOU KNOW if you are ever diagnosed with a brain tumor, you are NOT going to survive!"

Ten months later, when I was diagnosed with my first brain tumor, I had to eat my words.

YOUR "VICTORY?!" NOTES

_____

_____

_____

_____

_____

_____

_____

_____

_____

_____

_____

_____

_____

_____

YOUR "VICTORY?!" NOTES

Judy Lombardo

CHAPTER 15

FLYING

"I'm afraid to fly, and I don't know why," begins one of Marvin Hamlisch's songs in one of my favorite musicals, *"They're Playing Our Song"*.* Yes, I'm a theater nerd. I've also been afraid to fly for almost as long as I can remember. The first time I flew was the summer I was twelve. My dad, sister and I took a sight-seeing plane over Cape Cod. My dad intentionally picked a sunny day with calm winds to take us. He told us it would be fun. The purpose was so we could get a taste of flying before we flew to see our cousins in California the following summer. It was a four-seater plane, just the pilot and us. It was noisy! I also remember a rough landing. Other than that, I didn't care one way or the other for it.

The following summer, mom, dad, my sister and I flew from New York to Los Angeles to visit our cousins, go to Disneyland and other touristy southern California things. I don't remember it being a rough ride. However, I do remember staring out the window for five hours and looking at the ground wondering what was keeping us up in the air. I was just slightly scared then.

The next time I flew was going to my college orientation with my dad. I went to college seven hundred miles from home. So only the two of us went for my orientation. It was a very rough ride. I remember being scared even though my dad was calm. Suddenly a man sitting behind us started loudly singing, "Too-Ra-Loo-Ra-Loo-Ral." He sounded like one of the Irish Tenors. As he sang, the rest of the passengers went silent. There we were bouncing around on a plane in turbulence, with that song being sung beautifully. It was so eerie!

For the next four years I flew roundtrip for Thanksgiving, Christmas break, Spring Break and one way at the end of the school year. I had more than my share of rough rides and was just terrified every time I had to fly. I wanted so badly to go home, but I was scared to fly. Each time, I begged all my friends to pray for me and the flight. "Tell the pilot to be careful," one of my friends said trying to make me feel better.

Every time I was on a rough airplane ride, I would get severe dizzy spells, and I didn't know which way was up! I'd finally get my equilibrium back just in time for more turbulence. Being dizzy and not knowing which way was up, was terrifying for me. I couldn't think rationally under those conditions. But it never occurred to me, or my family, that I might have a brain tumor causing the pressure in my head to be so messed up.

I wanted so badly to go to college closer to home so I wouldn't have to fly. But my parents would not let me transfer. (It's a long story for another time). On December 20, 1988, I flew home for Christmas break of my senior year. The following night we were eating dinner in my parents' kitchen when the news came on saying Pan Am flight 103 had blown up over Scotland. There were 40 Syracuse students aboard. Less than an hour later I found out that one of those students on board was a high school classmate of mine. She and three other people from my hometown were on it. She was not a close friend, but it was way too close to home for me, as it was for all of who knew her. I was never going to fly again – which would mean I would miss my last semester of college. But my parents made me go back in January. I was shaking and crying the whole way back to school. I know that largely contributed to my fear of flying, but with or without that incident in the back of my mind, I was miserable on any flight that was not smooth.

So, what was I thinking when after college, I moved an additional one hundred miles away from home for my first job? I was thinking about my independence and a much cheaper cost of living. I was not thinking about flying. Nevertheless, for the next three years I flew "home" for holidays and once during the summer. Once, when I told my parents that I was going to drive home from Indianapolis, they strongly objected. So, I didn't tell them, and drove anyway. I called them from a pay phone at 10:00 p.m.

one summer night telling them I was down the street and to unlock the door. They were not happy that I drove eight hundred miles by myself. Oh well.

I continued to be miserable and dizzy on any flights with turbulence. My mother told me I was just oversensitive. But to me, it was one giant roller coaster ride. I hated roller coasters ever since I passed out on a kiddie coaster when I was six. On smooth flights I was fine. Not understanding why I was this way made my fear snowball into "anticipatory anxiety" as I was once told. My shakiness and fear would start twenty-four hours before I had to fly. People told me it was safe, and thought I was afraid to die. That wasn't it, I assured them. But no one believed me.

Christmas of 1992, my mom flew to Indianapolis to bring me back to Connecticut via flying. She said I would be fine since she was with me. I dreaded getting on that flight, but I went with my mom and I was miserable. When we landed, I overheard her tell my father, "Well, she made it, but didn't do too well. She was as white as a ghost." Remember that by that time I had been diagnosed with a brain tumor, but the doctor said I should be fine to fly.

What I remember about the first time I flew after my first brain surgery, was that I felt so much less pressure in my head and was able to relax on the trip. Maybe there wasn't much turbulence, but I don't remember anything other than feeling much better.

That feeling did not continue. To this day, I get very dizzy on flights that are turbulent. I even have to plan my trip so that I get a window seat and prop up my head against the window and do not move my head from that position while the plane levels off. Otherwise, the airplane turning up, down, left or right messes with my equilibrium.

As you read in Chapter 1, it was the fact that I was scheduled to fly home for Thanksgiving, that sent me to get an MRI, and accidentally discover I had a brain tumor. I credit going to college far from home and moving further away for my first job with saving my life. If I never had to get on that airplane for Thanksgiving in 1992, they would not have sent me for an MRI. Without the MRI, doctor after doctor kept sending me home saying I was fine or just had sinus issues.

*"They're Playing our Song" lyrics by *Carole Bayer Sager* and book by *Neil Simon*.

YOUR "VICTORY?!" NOTES

_____

_____

_____

_____

_____

_____

_____

_____

_____

_____

_____

_____

YOUR "VICTORY?!" NOTES

CHAPTER 16

WHY VICTORY?!

I originally planned on writing my story as a full-length book and I started to do so right after my first surgery in 1993. It was supposed to be sort of a catharsis. But I got so stressed out about it and upset, that I just couldn't do it then. It turned out to be more emotionally draining than ever. I just couldn't handle it that soon after I'd gone through it.

After Jackie, went through her ordeal, a neighbor of mine was diagnosed, and then, a friend of another family, who was only one and a half years old, was diagnosed. Then two friends of friends were diagnosed. "It's like an epidemic!" I thought. I had to get the word out, to inspire hope, to educate people on the subject. These days there are over two hundred new brain tumor/cancer diagnoses in the U.S. every day, and it is a subject that no one wants to talk about. We DO need to talk about it because it is becoming more and more prevalent, and there is no known way to prevent it or cure it! We have to inspire hope, educate the general public and make people realize that those of us who have had brain surgery are not freaks or some sort of Frankenstein-like experiment.

I HAD to do something! Other than donating money to research, and being supportive of other patients, writing a play and educating people is all I knew to do.

Then on January 4, 2012, exactly nineteen years to the day of my first brain surgery, I received notice from IndyFringe in Indianapolis, that my play had been accepted into the 2012 IndyFringe Festival. VICTORY!!!!!!

Today, I am having one of my, "Thank you God!" moments. To think that a survived all these struggles and now:

- It has been twenty-eight years since I survived my first brain tumor and craniotomy to remove it.
- I am a twenty-two-year brain tumor survivor from my second one and I continue to live with that second rock in my brain.
- I lived and felt well enough to write a one-woman show about my experiences and perform it in three states, including Hollywood, CA!
- In 2021, I entered an excerpt of this book in a "Write Your Story" contest with *Enhanced DNA Publishing* and won first place.
- I completed writing and publishing this full-length book, four months after winning that contest!

So, I ask you now, "Victory?!"
I say, "YES!"

YOUR "VICTORY?!" NOTES

_____

_____

_____

_____

_____

_____

_____

_____

_____

_____

_____

_____

_____

YOUR "VICTORY?!" NOTES

ABOUT THE AUTHOR

Judy Lombardo grew up in Stamford, Connecticut where her mother's side of the family had lived since the 1680's. Judy is the proud daughter of Ann and Tom, two public elementary school educators and older sister of Kathy.

Judy received her Bachelor of Science degree in Mass Communications, from Miami University in Oxford, Ohio. She then got her first professional job in Indianapolis, Indiana where she has now lived for more than thirty years.

Judy loves theatre, dogs, UCONN basketball, sit-coms and ALL people of good will.

Judy Lombardo

REFERENCES

https://www.abta.org/about-brain-tumors/brain-tumor-education/

For more information about brain tumors, both benign and malignant, go to the American Brain Tumor Association website:

https://www.abta.org/

or call or email

800-886-2282
info@abta.org

Judy Lombardo

Denola M. Burton
www.EnhancedDNAPublishing.com
DenolaBurton@EnhancedDNA1.com

Made in the USA
Columbia, SC
19 July 2021